MW01608116

RYAN MILLIGAN

LET'S INVESTIGATE

CONJURING

Published in this edition by Peter Haddock Ltd, Pinfold Lane,
Bridlington, East Yorkshire YO16 5BT

ISBN 0 7105 0966 9

Printed and bound in India

PART ONE

A FEW SIMPLE TRICKS

How does one become a conjuror? The answer to this question is very simple. You learn how to perform a few simple tricks well then go out and find yourself an audience. It does not matter whether it be of only one person, or a few members of your family, or a group at the local youth club, or even several hundred people at the annual school concert, so long as there is someone who is prepared to watch you perform.

Once you have performed your tricks for an audience, you have become a conjuror. You may not be a very good conjuror yet, but you are a conjuror. So, should you decide that you wish to become a conjuror, the first project is to learn a few simple magic tricks. How does one learn a few magic tricks? There are several answers to this question, and most of them depend on what type of performance would suit you best.

Broadly speaking, a magic act can consist of the following:

Sleight-of-hand tricks—those that are dependent on the skill and dexterity of the performer.

Mind-reading tricks—those in which the performer apparently reads the minds of his or her spectators.

Mechanical tricks—those that require no skill or dexterity on the part of the performer. The term 'mechanical' is one that is often used by conjurors to describe a trick that is easy to do or is dependent on some secret device to make it work.

Stage illusions—usually of a very large nature, which require several assistants who are specially trained for the job.

For the beginner, mechanical tricks are the best. So start with a mechanical trick.

Project

The torn and restored newspaper trick

This is a trick you can make up for yourself and will cost you practically nothing. Unfold a double sheet of newspaper and tear it into several pieces. Hold the pieces at arm's length in front of the body, then start to unfold them, and the audience will see that the pieces have become magically restored to the full-size sheet of newspaper again.

The secret of this trick is that two identical sheets of newspaper are used.

To prepare for this trick you will need the two sheets of newspaper, some glue or paste and a rubber band. Take one sheet of paper and fold it up, as illustrated in figure 1. Once it has been folded, the newspaper should measure about 7.5 centimetres (3 inches) square. Place the rubber band around this packet.

Open out the other sheet of paper and lay it on a flat surface. Smear a dab of paste on the paper at the point marked X in figure 1. Take the small packet and place it on the paste and press it down firmly and leave it to dry. It would probably be a good idea to make up several of these papers and leave them to dry so that you will have a number of them ready to practise with. Once the paste is dry, fold the sheet up with the small packet inside.

To perform the trick. Pick the newspaper up from your table and unfold it carefully, making sure that the side that has the small packet stuck to it is on the side nearest to you and away from the audience. Tear the newspaper into two. Place the two pieces together so that the small packet is still nearest to your body. In other words, always hold the piece of newspaper that contains the small packet in the right hand and always place the pieces in the left hand in front of those in the right, on the side nearest to the audience. If you continue to tear up the newspaper you will finish up with a lot of small pieces of newspaper about three inches square and behind them, unknown to the audience, is another sheet of newspaper folded up into a small packet.

Hold them up about chest high in front of your body. Place both thumbs under the rubber band and lift it

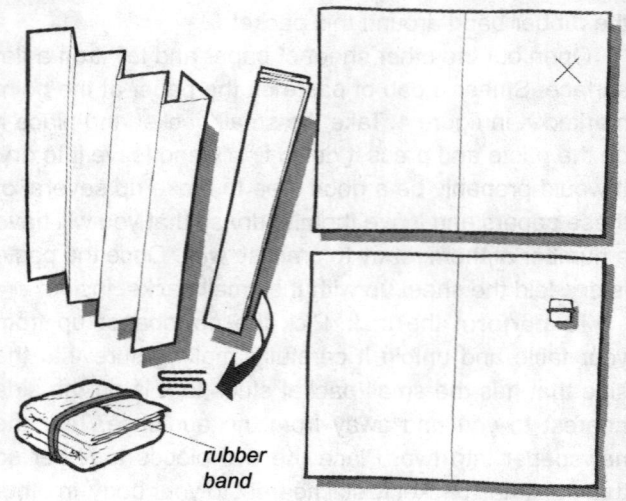

Figure 1

upwards and off the packet and over the small pieces. Turn the packet over so that the torn pieces are on the side nearest to you and the small packet is at the front facing the audience.

UNFOLD THE PACKET

At this point it might be a good idea to explain that the rubber band is now holding the torn pieces together and the small packet is now free to be unfolded. You now start to unfold the small packet, and the audience will see that the small pieces have become magically restored to one large sheet. As you unfold the small packet, be careful to keep the side with the torn pieces held to it by the rubber band, away from the audience.

If you are performing this on a large stage you could probably use any rubber band, but if you are performing it in a smaller room it would be advisable to use a white rubber band so that it would blend in with the newspaper and remain unseen.

One last word of warning. Do not ever perform this effect with a light shining behind you. The light will shine through the newspaper and cause the torn pieces to cast a shadow through the paper.

Project

Try the vanishing wand trick

The vanishing wand is an excellent trick with which to open your magic show. Walk to centre stage carrying a magic wand in your right hand. After making your opening remarks, tap your magic wand on the table top to prove, without saying so, that it is what it appears to be, a solid magic wand. Picking up a piece of tissue paper from your table, proceed to wrap the wand up in the paper. Once more, after the wand has been wrapped, tap it on your table top. Now hold the wand, still wrapped in paper, in both hands in front of your body. Suddenly crush the paper up into a ball and toss it aside. The magic wand has vanished. Slowly reach into your inside breast pocket and bring forth the magic wand.

The secret—a glance at the illustrations in figure 2 will reveal all. The magic wand that you are holding in your hand when you enter is not what it appears to be.

To prepare. It is simply a paper tube made from black flint paper, with two solid wooden ends painted white inserted in the ends of the tube. A spot of glue will hold the ends firmly in place. If you hold this 'wand' by one end you can tap the other end on the table to prove that it is solid. After it has been wrapped in tissue paper it

Figure 2

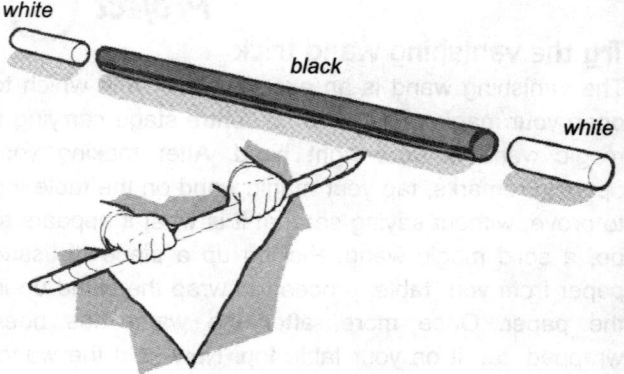

is a very simple matter to crush the wand up inside the paper apparently making it vanish.

Do not forget to retrieve your ends, or 'wand tips' as they are called, after the show; you will need them again for your next performance.

The wand that is taken from your pocket after the 'vanish' has been placed there before you make your entrance. It should be about 30 centimetres (12 inches) long by 1.5 centimetres ($\frac{1}{2}$ inch) in diameter. Made from a wooden rod, it should be painted black in the centre and 4 centimetres ($1\frac{1}{2}$ inches) at both ends should be painted white.

The solid wand and the trick wand should look exactly alike.

MAGIC READING

Now that you have two magic tricks at your command, are there others? Yes, there are thousands of them. Once you start on a project such as this, you suddenly develop a thirst for knowledge, and the best place to acquire knowledge of any subject is usually in a book. Where does one find a book of magic? Practically every public library has a small section devoted to books about magic. Usually they are tucked away in some obscure corner of the library, but if you cannot find them just ask the librarian. Occasionally there may be a particular book you would like to read but you cannot find it on the shelves of your local library. In this case, ask the librarian if it is possible for a copy to be obtained. It is his or her job to buy books for members of the public. If public funds will allow it, and the librarian thinks that the book will be of interest to others in the community, he or she will order it.

HISTORY OF MAGIC

It is from books that you will learn the history of magic. You will read of magicians of the past, learn their secrets, develop a 'feel' for magic. You will read of Chung Ling Soo, the great Chinese illusionist who was tragically shot dead on stage in full view of an audience while attempting to catch a bullet in his teeth.

You will read of Cardini, the greatest sleight of hand performer the world has ever known. Cardini specialised in the manipulation of playing cards, lighted cigarettes and full-size billiard balls. Wherever Cardini appeared, magicians flocked to see him, in top hat, white tie and tails, with a monocle and cigarette holder. These were his trademarks. Packs of playing cards appeared from nowhere to the bewilderment of the audience. Lighted cigarettes appeared and disappeared, changed to cigars and finally a pipe. Billiard balls changed colour and suddenly multiplied. This was truly magic.

THE GREATEST SHOWMAN

You will read of Houdini, the greatest showman the world has ever known. He would be tied hand and foot, manacled, strapped in a straitjacket, suspended upside down from a crane, but from all these restraints he would walk away in the twinkling of an eye. Then there are Thurston, Kellar, Blackstone, Dante, Lyle, Lafayette, John Henry Anderson, the Wizard of the North, Carmo, Maskelyne—we could go on forever naming great magicians of the past. Pinetti, Robert Houdin—the French magician from whom Houdini took his name—Cagliostro, Torrini, Chefalo, John Mulholland.

From books you will learn secrets that have been forgotten by others. You will read about more recent magicians—Channing Pollok from the US, Silvan from Italy, Ken Littlewood from Australia, David Bamberg, a 7th-generation magician from South America, The Great Wong from Singapore, the ever popular Paul Daniels from the UK and the sophisticated American conjurer, David Copperfield. Big magicians, small magicians, nightclub magicians, and all with one thing in common, a love of magic. You can read all about them in your public library.

MAGIC COLLECTORS

You will learn about the magic collectors. People who

collect posters, theatre programmes, books, photographs, equipment that was used by famous magicians of the past, anything that has a bearing on magic. You will discover that there have been and still are magical historians. You will read of people like Milbourne Christopher, Jay Marshall, Jimmy Findlay, and many others. People who are continually digging very deeply into the past to discover and rediscover secrets, knowledge, information, anything that will shed another light one of the most fascinating subjects in the world.

THE WORLD OF MAGIC

The very first time you make a coin disappear or perform a simple card trick, you become a part of this world, the world of magic. But first you need knowledge. There are many different types of magic, and you have been shown the vanishing wand and the torn and restored newspaper tricks, both of which are of a mechanical nature in that no great skill is required to perform either of them.

PART TWO

SLEIGHT OF HAND

The basic requirement of all conjurors who aspire to being sleight of hand experts is simple. Two hands with five fingers on each hand. They need not be long and slender, any ten fingers will do. Two things are possible in a sleight of hand performance. You can make things appear or you can make things disappear. If you make an object change its appearance, such as changing a red billiard ball into a white billiard ball, all you have really done is make the red billiard ball disappear and make the white billiard ball appear in its place. The combination of the appearance and the disappearance gives you another effect—a change. As you progress you will discover that by combining two effects it is possible to create a third, and different, effect.

Project

Make a coin disappear

Start with something that almost everyone has in his or her pocket, a few coins. How do you make a coin disappear? Simple. Hold the coin as in figure 3 in your left hand. Bring your right hand up and place your right fingers in front of the coin and your right thumb behind

Figure 3

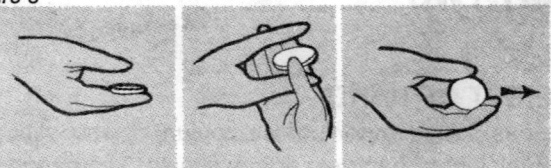

the coin. Now relax the left fingers and allow the coin to drop backwards on to the left fingers. At the same time, lift your right hand upwards as if it held the coin, drop the left hand to your side, still secretly holding the coin. Close your right hand into a fist and squeeze it gently and open the hand slowly. The coin has vanished. Follow the illustrations through from figure 3, slowly at first so that you get used to it and then just a little faster but not quickly.

A DIFFERENT EFFECT

Now that you can make a coin disappear, here is a different effect using the same sleight of hand. Look again at the illustrations and notice how the coin has fallen on to the fingers of the left hand. This position is called the finger palm. Right? Now hold a coin in the left hand in the same position as before, but this time, unknown to your spectators, you have another coin of a different value concealed in the finger palm position in the right hand. Go through the same movements as before—bring the right hand up to the left hand and apparently take the coin in the right hand but really letting it drop back on to the fingers of the left hand. The right hand moves away apparently holding the coin. The left hand drops to your side. The right hand moves away, closes into a fist and squeezes gently. The right hand is opened and the spectators see another coin. You have performed a change, and it was your first sleight of hand trick. The same effect can be performed with buttons or anything similar.

Project

The multiplying billiard balls

Now we come to something a little more ambitious. Although this trick is normally done with billiard balls, you need not necessarily use them. Table tennis balls will do. This is a real classic of magic. We will explain at the end of this effect how you can make your own equipment with table tennis balls but would suggest that you try to acquire the proper equipment. Really first class professional quality multiplying billiard balls can be expensive, but it is also possible to get a small-sized beginner's set quite cheaply.

The effect is as follows. Hold a red ball at arm's length between your forefinger and thumb. Give the ball a shake, and another one appears between your forefinger and middle finger. Knock the two balls together to prove they are solid, and place the balls back between the fingers of the right hand. Give them a shake, and a third ball appears. Tapping all three balls, place them back into the right fingers, give them one more shake, and still another ball, making four, appears in the fingers of your right hand. Drop all four balls, one at a time, into a hat or box that is sitting on the table.

The secret. In fact, there are only three and a half balls used. The half ball, known as a 'shell', will fit over any one of the three balls. Figure 4 shows this.

To prepare. Place two billiard balls in your left trouser pocket. The third ball with the shell over it is in a hat or box on the table.

PERFORM THE EFFECT

Pick the ball up from the table, holding it between the forefinger and thumb and keeping the shell in place on the ball. The shell should be on the side of the ball that is nearest to the audience. Place the middle finger under the ball and roll it upwards out of the shell. From the front it will look as if you have two complete billiard balls.

While you were multiplying one ball into two, your left hand should be placed into your trouser pocket secretly to get hold of one of the two balls that are there. Once you have multiplied one ball to two, your left hand is

Figure 4

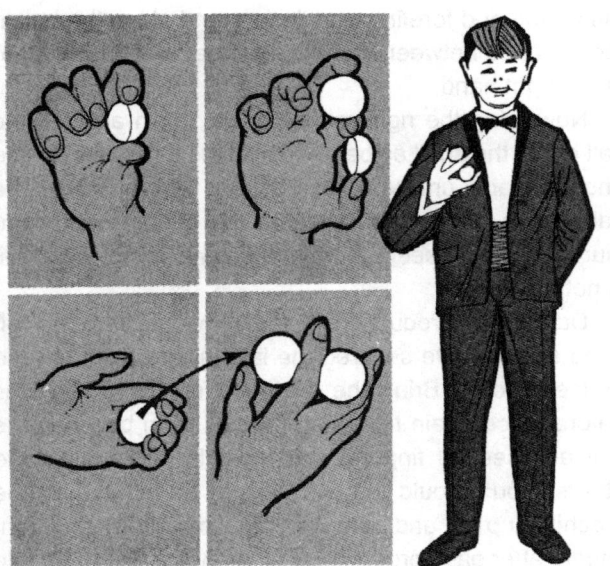

removed from your pocket, still holding the ball, with the back of the left hand to the audience. It reaches up to the right hand, removes the ball and, as it does so, the left hand leaves the ball it is holding inside the shell.

THE SHELL

You are now apparently holding one billiard ball in each hand, but unknown to the audience the ball in the right hand has a shell over it. Hold this ball and shell between the thumb and forefinger as before and place the ball in the left hand between the middle finger and fourth finger of the right hand.

Now bring the right middle finger down and roll the ball out of the shell as before. This time it may feel a little uncomfortable until you have done it several times. The ball that is being held between the middle finger and fourth finger will seem to be in the way. Do not worry—it is not too difficult.

During the production of the previous ball, the left hand should have secured the last billiard ball from the trouser pocket. Bring the left hand up to the right as before, once again removing the ball from between the first and second fingers, and tap this ball against the others. You should have realised by now that the reaching up to and removal of a ball from the right fingers after each production is merely a cover to enable you to place another ball into the shell.

You should now have reached the position of having three balls in the right hand with the shell on the one being held by the forefinger and thumb, the other balls having been placed between the middle and fourth fingers and the fourth and little finger.

Once again the middle finger comes downwards and rolls the ball upwards out of the shell. It now looks as if you have four billiard balls held in the right fingers. Lower the hand and drop the billiard balls one at a time, starting with the shell, into a hat or box on your table.

If you cut a table tennis ball in half, it will almost fit over another ball. This is not quite as satisfactory as the proper set from a magic dealer, but they are a good substitute.

THE MAGIC DEALERS

We have not as yet mentioned the magic dealer. This is one aspect of the magic scene that is not too well known to the public at large. The magic dealers are men and women who specialise in the manufacture of equipment for conjurors. In these places it is possible to buy anything from a trick pack of cards to a complete sawing-a-person-in-half outfit. To anyone who wants to be a conjuror, the magic dealer can be a very good friend indeed. He or she can recommend the right tricks for certain audiences, tell you where there are magicians performing locally, and the best books to read.

MIRROR BOX

This is a very popular trick that is sold by most magic dealers. It is a box that can be shown to be empty at any time and yet a number of handkerchiefs, ribbons, sweets, etc, can be produced from within it.

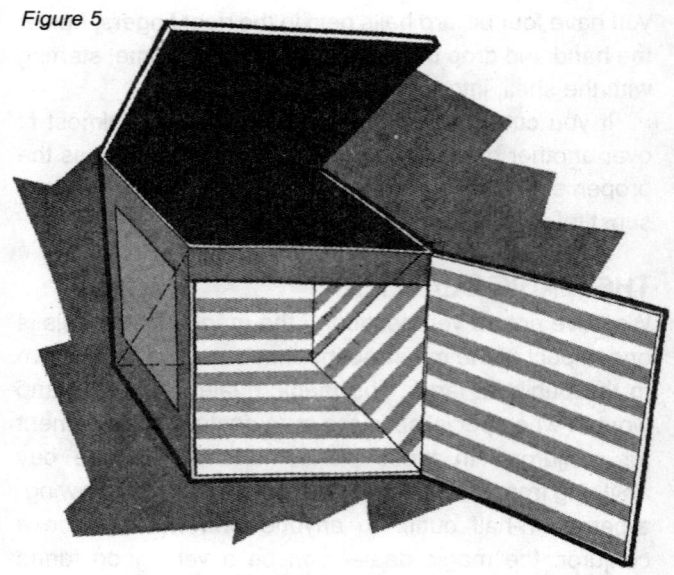

Figure 5

Figure 5 will make everything clear. The mirror is placed into the box at an angle of 45 degrees. If the front door is opened, the spectators can see into the box, and it will appear to be empty because they will see the bottom of the box reflected in the mirror and they will assume that they can see the whole of the inside of the box. If the front door is now closed and the lid of the box is opened, you can now produce your handkerchiefs or whatever you wish to use for your trick.

cats and rats, each with teeth as big as bananas, chewing huge holes wherever they went; I dreamt of an ogre with false teeth so enormous he kept them in a bucket on his bedside table; I dreamt that every kid in the world had teeth the size of elephant tusks and when they fell out the tooth-fairy needed a fork-lift truck to carry them away.

The dream was so scary it woke me up. For a while I lay there all of a tremble while my heart went thump-thump-thump and my mouth felt stuffed with cobwebs. Maybe I needed a drink of water. Quickly I slipped out of bed to go downstairs. I'd forgotten all about the tooth-fairy trap. *Kerplonk! Kerfuffle! Kapow!*

There I was in the moonlight with my feet jammed in an umbrella, my head stuck fast in a birdcage and the rest of me tangled up in a muddle of elastic, glue, vinegar and brown paper, two walking-sticks, an old fishing-rod and three coat-hangers bent out of shape. To tell you the truth I felt a bit of a wally when the light was switched on.

'Whatever's the matter?' said Mum and Dad and my Big Brother.

'Nothing,' I said. 'I'm just waiting for the tooth-fairy. He hasn't been yet.'

'Hasn't he?' said my Big Brother.

From under my pillow he pulled a crumpled note and a ten-pence piece. The note said,

SORRY ABOUT THE TRAP IT'S YOUR OWN FAULT FOR TRYING TO TRICK A NIFTY PERSON LIKE ME

Only the writing wasn't in capital letters any more — it was a loose, wobbly, toothy sort of writing.

'You've got to admit the tooth-fairy is pretty nifty,' laughed Big Brother.

'Very nifty,' I said gloomily.

Any day now, though, my second tooth will drop out. Then we'll really see how nifty the tooth-fairy is.

EATING ICE CREAM WITH
A WEREWOLF
by Phyllis Green

When Brad and Fat Nancy's parents go to Bermuda, they need a baby-sitter at short notice.

'Not Phoebe Hadley,' Brad pleaded. 'She almost drowned me once, and last time she baby-sat, I ended up in hospital. She always has a hobby she wants to try out on me. Please, anyone, but not Phoebe Hadley.'

But Mum and Dad were talking about Bermuda and Brad couldn't get a word in edgeways. All he could do was wait until Phoebe arrived . . .

Zany, outrageous Phoebe turned her stay into the most hilarious adventure Brad and Nancy had ever had; they never knew *what* was going to happen next! What could have caused the chicken to appear on Nancy's bed? Did they *really* eat ice cream with a werewolf?

0 552 524190

CORGI

TOM'S SAUSAGE LION
by Michael Morpurgo

It was Christmas Eve when Tom first saw the
lion. His mother had sent him out to fetch logs –
and there was the lion padding through the
orchard with a string of sausages in its mouth!
Tom couldn't believe his eyes and, worst still,
when he rushed indoors to tell them, his family
didn't believe him either.

There *was* a lion. Tom knew there was, knew
that he hadn't dreamed it. So he sat up, night
after night, waiting for the lion to return . . .

0 552 524182

Available soon from Corgi Books

MANY HAPPY RETURNS AND OTHER STORIES
by Kathryn Cave

Alice loathes all her birthday presents on sight and finds a hilarious way of dealing with them . . .

Cousin Roderick comes to stay and causes chaos until a spider provides an unusual solution . . .

The dreaded Mrs Bannerman terrorizes her class when mystery messages from 'Billy Molloy' appear on the blackboard. Who wrote them?

And just what *are* James and Mary going to do about the dinosaur in their garden?

These are just a few of the extremely funny and perceptive stories in this new collection from Kathryn Cave, author of the highly popular *Dragonrise*.

0 552 524344

Available soon from Corgi Books

If you would like to receive a Newsletter about our new Children's books, just fill in the coupon below with your name and address (or copy it onto a separate piece of paper if you don't want to spoil your book) and send it to:

The Children's Books Editor
Young Corgi Books
61–63 Uxbridge Road
Ealing
London W5 5SA

Please send me a Children's Newsletter:

Name ....

Address..

....

....

All Children's Books are available at your bookshop or newsagent, or can be ordered from the following address:

Corgi/Bantam Books,
Cash Sales Department,
P.O. Box 11, Falmouth, Cornwall TR10 9EN

Please send a cheque or postal order (no currency) and allow 60p for postage and packing for the first book plus 25p for the second book and 15p for each additional book ordered up to a maximum charge of £1.90 in UK.

B.F.P.O. customers please allow 60p for the first book, 25p for the second book plus 15p per copy for the next 7 books, thereafter 9p per book.

Overseas customers, including Eire, please allow £1.25 for postage and packing for the first book, 75p for the second book, and 28p for each subsequent title ordered.

Project

Make your own mirror box

The best size for the mirror box is 11 x 11 x 11 centimetres (4^1/$_2$ x 4^1/$_2$ x 4^1/$_2$ inches). If you cut six squares of cardboard 11 x 11 centimetres (4^1/$_2$ x 4^1/$_2$ inches), cover them on both sides with a patterned wallpaper by means of a brush and a jar of paste, you can now build up the box and seal it together with coloured sticky tape, 2.5 centimetres (1 inch) wide. Notice that the lid of the box is hinged at the back and the front door is hinged down one side. Before attaching the front door to the box, place a strip of card, also covered with the same wallpaper, across the top front edge of the box and tape it at both ends to the box. This strip, which should be 11 x 2 centimetres (4^1/$_2$ x ^{3}/$_4$ inches) serves a double purpose. First, it keeps the two sides of the box in position, and secondly it hides the front edge of the mirror at the top.

For the mirror, you could use a real glass mirror, but would probably have to get an expert to cut it for you, because glass cutting is a tricky business. The easiest way is to buy a small sheet of flexi-mirror. This is a plastic that is quite thin and is very easily cut with a pair of household scissors or even a penknife and is a perfect mirror. Cut a piece of this, measuring 16.5 x 11 centimetres (6^1/$_2$ x 4^1/$_2$ inches), and paste it to a piece of cardboard exactly the same size, which will strengthen it

25

because it is very thin, and insert it into the box, as shown in figure 5.

Did you notice that the wallpaper used in figure 5 has lines running across it? If you run the lines in the same direction as the mirror, the edges of the mirror will blend into the pattern of the paper, remain unseen, and add to the illusion that the box is empty.

Project

A trick with your mirror box

Fill the box's upper compartment with your handkerchiefs or ribbons. Having done this, place the box on your table with its back to your audience. Pick up the box and place it on your left hand. Open the front door, which should be facing you and not your audience, and then, after you have opened the front door, turn the box around so that the audience can see inside it. Turn the box around so that the front door is facing you again, close the front door of the box, and pick up your magic wand and wave it over the box. Place the magic wand back on the table, open the lid of the box and make your production.

AN OPTICAL ILLUSION

Before we leave the subject of mirrors, there is another use for your plastic mirror. Cut a piece of this mirror so that it will fit inside a glass. It need not be an exact fit and

Figure 6

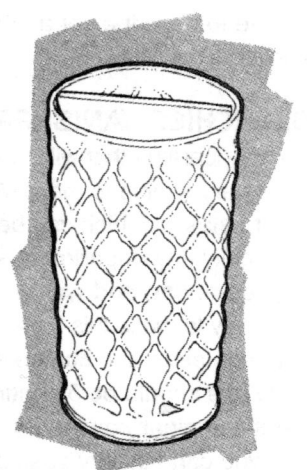

is perhaps best if it is a little too large. Because the mirror is pliable, it will bend a little as you push it into the glass. Use a glass that is not perfectly clear, one with an outside pattern on it. Once you have inserted the mirror into the glass, push a coloured handkerchief down behind the mirror. Place the glass on a table, with the handkerchief on the side of the mirror away from you, and step back a few feet. You will be amazed to discover that the glass looks perfectly empty. It is a beautiful optical illusion.

This magic prop, for that is indeed what it is, is called a 'mirror glass', and to enable you to use this in a magic show we will have to describe yet another item that is in every magician's bag of tricks.

THE HANDKERCHIEF VANISHER

This is a piece of apparatus that will make a handkerchief disappear and is very simple to make. All that is required is a length of cord elastic, which can be bought for a few pennies in practically any department store, and a small tube that is closed at one end with a hole drilled in the end. The easiest way to make this tube is to get hold of an aluminium cigar container and cut the end off. The piece you are going to use should be 5 centimetres (2 inches) long. Because these cigar containers are made of very thin aluminium, you can actually push a nail into the end to make a hole. If you have a small drill at home, it will, of course, make a much neater job.

Having drilled the hole in the end of the tube, thread the cord elastic through the hole and tie several knots in it to prevent it slipping back through the hole. Tie a loop at the other end of the elastic, which should be about 30 centimetres (12 inches) long, and you are ready to practise.

In figure 7 you will see a quick, cheap way of making a handkerchief vanisher by using an old salt cellar. Remove the screw bottom, thread the elastic through as before and 'Presto'—a handkerchief vanisher.

Fix the loop on the end of the elastic to your back

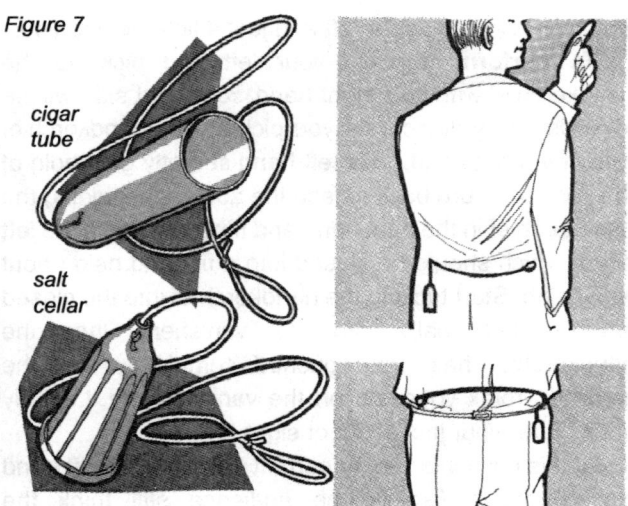

Figure 7

cigar
tube

salt
cellar

trouser button. If you wear a belt, use a safety pin to attach it at the back of your trousers. Take the vanisher and bring it around your waist to the front, then attach a safety pin to your trousers just above the pocket. The vanisher should hang just above the pocket. If it is hanging too low, then shorten the length of the elastic.

Project

Make the handkerchief vanish

To prepare for this effect, place a handkerchief, one small enough to be pushed into the vanisher, on your table, which should be to your left and just a little behind you.

To perform. Turn to your left and pick up the handkerchief with your right hand. Your right side will be towards the audience. As you pick up the handkerchief with your right hand, your left hand secretly gets hold of the vanisher. Turn back to face the audience, holding the handkerchief in the right hand and the vanisher in the left hand, which should be closed into a fist and held about waist high. Start tucking the handkerchief into the closed left fist but really into the vanisher. Once the handkerchief has been pushed completely into the vanisher, relax your grip on the vanisher and it will fly back under your jacket out of sight.

At this point it is very important to keep your left hand closed into a fist as the audience still think the handkerchief is in the left hand. Show the right hand empty, then lift the left hand up to shoulder height and open it with the palm facing the audience. This hand is now also empty. The handkerchief has vanished.

Project

Combine two tricks

Can you guess how we combine the handkerchief vanisher with the mirror glass? The plot is simple. Show the glass empty, vanish the handkerchief and then reproduce the handkerchief from the glass. To do this you require two handkerchiefs exactly alike, say green, and one other handkerchief, which should be of a different colour, say red. This should be large enough to cover the mirror glass completely when the glass is sitting on the table.

To prepare, conceal one green handkerchief in the glass behind the mirror and place the glass on your table with the mirror, of course, facing the audience. The red handkerchief should be folded up on the table, behind the mirror glass. The second green handkerchief should be lying on the table alongside the glass.

Perform the effect. Start by picking up the glass in your left hand and explaining that you are going to perform a little mystery with a glass—which you place back on the table—and this handkerchief, displaying the green handkerchief that is lying on the table.

Pick up the red handkerchief by the two corners and use it to cover the mirror glass completely. You should be standing behind your table at this point. Once you have covered the glass, walk round to the front of the table and pick up the green handkerchief with your right hand.

It is at this point that your left hand secures the handkerchief vanisher.

Proceed to vanish the handkerchief, as already described. Once you have made the handkerchief disappear, pick up the mirror glass from the table, still

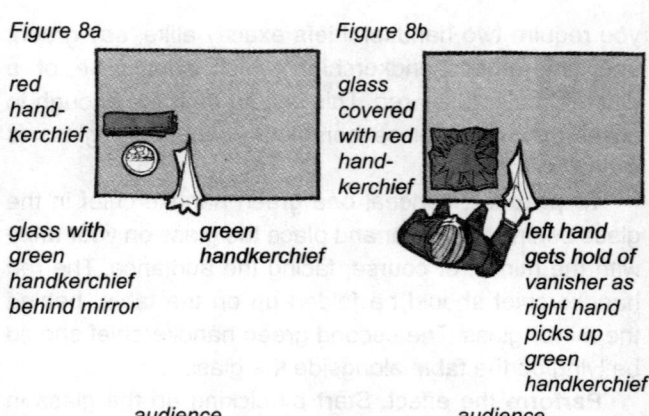

Figure 8a

red
hand-
kerchief

glass with
green
handkerchief
behind mirror

green
handkerchief

audience

Figure 8b

glass
covered
with red
hand-
kerchief

left hand
gets hold of
vanisher as
right hand
picks up
green
handkerchief

audience

covered by the red handkerchief, and place it on the left hand. As you do this, turn the glass around so that the handkerchief inside the glass comes to the front of the glass. Holding the glass in the left hand, lift the red handkerchief off the glass with the right hand, and the audience will see that the green handkerchief is now inside the glass. They will assume, of course, that this is the same handkerchief that disappeared so mysteriously from your hands a moment before.

PART THREE

CHEMICAL MAGIC

Various chemicals are used in a vast number of magic tricks, and although many of these effects are simple to perform, some of them are very effective indeed.

THE UPSY-DOWNSY MOTHBALLS

Very simply, the effect is that you have a litre size cordial bottle, full of water, sitting on your table. You drop two or three mothballs into the top of the bottle, and they will mysteriously begin to float from the top to the bottom of the bottle and back up again. This will go on indefinitely and is fascinating to watch.

The secret is that the 'water' is not really water. It is a chemical preparation that only you will know about.

To prepare for this effect, you take four teaspoonfuls of bicarbonate of soda, and four teaspoonfuls of citric acid crystals and mix them together in a large jug. Pour one litre of water into the jug on top of the mixture and it will suddenly foam up for a minute or so. Once it has settled down, pour the liquid into a litre bottle. All that remains now is for you to drop the mothballs into the bottle of 'water', sit back and watch the show. Do not discard this as just a novelty. It looks spooky.

We have explained the upsy-downsy mothballs to illustrate the fact that there are a number of things that happen quite naturally but of which the general public has no knowledge, so the conjuror can make use of these principles to create a magic effect.

Figure 9

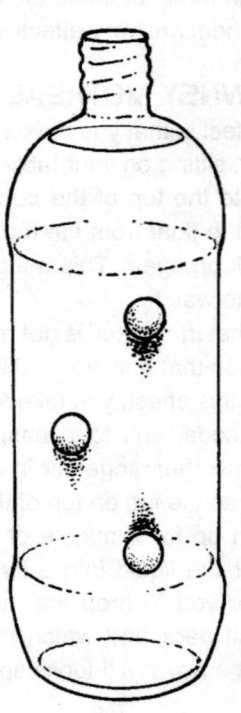

Practise the wine and water trick

The effect is because of the behaviour of certain chemicals in relation to others. Four glasses, all empty, are sitting on a tray. Also on the tray is a large jug of water. The water is poured into the glasses. In two of the glasses, the water remains clear. In the other two glasses, the water turns a bright red colour. When the two glasses of 'red' water are poured back into the jug of water, all the water in the jug turns red. The two glasses holding the clear water are now poured back into the jug, and all the contents of the jug now turn back into clear water.

To prepare. No doubt by now you have realised that the 'water' is not really water at all. All that is required to perform this effect is a tray that is large enough to hold four glasses—the glasses could either be quarter litre tumblers or wine glasses—and a jug that will hold enough liquid to fill all four glasses.

You will also require the following chemicals, all of which can be bought from most chemist shops: tartaric acid, bicarbonate of soda, phenolphthalein. The first two are powders and the third a clear liquid.

Line the four glasses up in a row on the tray. Into the first one, reading from left to right, place a few drops of phenolphthalein. Into the second glass, place some tartaric acid. Into the third a few drops of phenolphthalein, and into the fourth a few grains of tartaric acid.

Into the jug of water you mix some bicarbonate of soda. The jug of water will still have the same appearance and still look like water.

To perform. If you pour this 'water' into the first glass it will still remain clear. If you pour it into the second glass it will turn red (wine?), into the third, clear again, and into the last glass it will turn red.

You now take the two red glasses and pour them into the jug (which should still have some liquid in it), and the whole lot will turn to red. You now take the two glasses holding the clear liquid and pour them into the jug, and everything will turn back to clear water.

This is a very spectacular and colourful effect. A very good patter theme for this is to talk about soldiers who were drinking in their barrack room when the sergeant caught them, and one soldier said:

'What, us drinking? Don't be daft, Sarge, it's just water. Look!'

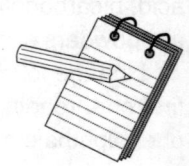

PART FOUR

CARD TRICKS
The wizard's pack of cards

This is one of the most useful weapons in the armoury of the conjuror. In appearance, it looks exactly like any other pack of cards but in fact it is designed to enable the conjuror to remain one step ahead of his or her audience.

The whole secret of this pack lies in the fact that one end is narrower than the other. In other words, the cards are tapered a little at one end, and 'little' in this case is the operative word. It would be impossible to sit down and cut the cards with a pair of scissors, but if you have a friend who is an amateur photographer, ask him or her if you can borrow a photograph trimmer. The edge of any pack of cards can be trimmed in a few minutes.

A piece of stout cardboard can be fixed to the trimmer with sticky tape and will act as your straight edge, ensuring that every card in the pack is trimmed exactly alike (*see* figure 10). Notice that it has been fixed at a slight angle. Some of the more expensive photographic trimmers have fittings that would enable you to trim the cards at an angle, but if yours does not have these fittings, the piece of cardboard will do.

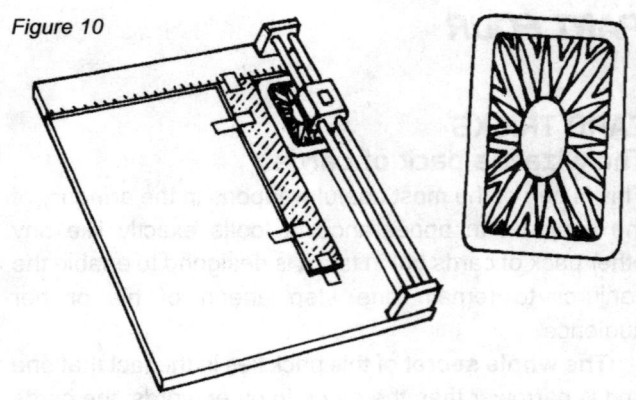

Figure 10

After the cards have been trimmed, you will notice that you have lost part of the corner of the cards. All corners of playing cards are rounded, but after you have trimmed the cards you will have one corner that is not rounded. Just snip the sharp corner away with a pair of nail scissors, leaving a rounded corner from the shape of the clippers.

Project

Operate the cards

There are perhaps over one hundred different tricks that can be performed with the aid of the wizard's pack of cards, and once you have understood the working of the pack you will be able to make your own tricks up with its aid.

To operate the cards, have someone select a card from the pack. Ask him or her to look at and remember the name of the card. As you are talking, turn the pack around in your hands, end for end. Ask the spectator to push the card back into the pack and to shuffle the cards.

Take the cards back from the spectator. To find the card, all you have to do is run your finger and thumb down the sides of the pack and the spectator's card will be pulled out of the pack.

By turning the pack around, after the spectator has selected the card, and then having the card pushed back into the pack, you have ensured that the wide end of the spectator's card is at the narrow end of the pack. Slide your finger and thumb down the sides of the pack and the card can be pulled out.

You will probably realise that if this can be done with one card, it can also be done with several cards. Reverse the four aces in the deck, placing their wide ends at the narrow end of the pack. Give the pack to anyone to shuffle, and when it is returned to you, hold the pack behind your back for a second then bring forth the four aces. Again, it is simply a matter of sliding your finger and thumb down the sides of the pack and the four aces will almost pop out of the pack into your fingers.

Project

Separate the colours

Still another effective trick that can be done only with the aid of this pack is the Colour Separation. To perform this trick, all the red cards in the pack must be turned around so that the wide ends of the red cards are at the other end of the pack from the wide ends of all the black cards. Have someone shuffle the cards and hand them back to you. Once again, all you have to do is place the cards behind your back, and, holding the pack by forefinger and thumb at each end, pull the red cards out in one hand and the black cards in the other (see figure 11).

Figure 11

PART FIVE

MIND-READING TRICKS

To be able to read a person's mind has been the secret dream of humans for centuries. So far, no one has ever really done this, but magicians have, by subtle means, been able to make people think that they can read people's minds.

Here is one of the oldest tricks of this nature, and one that used to be known to most schoolboys. Ask a friend of yours to do the following simple sum in his or her head. Stress the fact that your friend does not write anything down and that it is all done 'in the mind'.

Ask your friend to think of a number.

Double it.

Add eight.

Halve it.

Subtract the number he or she first thought of from this total.

Your friend will be surprised when you tell him or her that the number he or she is now thinking of is four. If you go through the above sequence, you will realise that the number your friend is left with is actually half of the number you asked him or her to add at stage three. Because your friend has done all of this in his or her head, you will create the effect of having read his or her mind. If you had asked your friend to add fourteen, the final answer would have been seven, again half of the number you had asked him or her to add at stage three.

Another very simple but very effective trick of a mind-reading nature is to reach into your pocket, bring out a handful of coins and ask a spectator to pick one of them, look at its date and remember it. You then apparently concentrate very hard and say, 'The date you are thinking of is 1982,' and you are right. How? Simple, all the coins in your pocket have the same date. Now you may not think this is very subtle, but if you have a friend who is a confederate and he or she has a number of coins that all have the same date and you ask the other person to look at one of the coins in your friend's pocket, then you have something that really appears to be mind reading.

Project

Turn yourself into a computer

Magic Numbers is an effect in which you appear to have a mind as fast as a computer.

Write down on a sheet of paper the numbers 12,345,679. Ask someone to give you any single digit. Suppose they say 5. You immediately ask them to multiply the number 12,345,679 by 45. When they do so they will get the answer 555,555,555. In other words, whatever number they give you, the final answer will consist of nothing else but that number. If you follow the above instance it will be as follows:

$$
\begin{array}{r}
12,345,679 \\
\underline{45} \\
61,728,395 \\
\underline{493,827,160} \\
555,555,555
\end{array}
$$

The secret to this one is also very simple. Multiply whatever number they give you by 9. So, if they say 4, you tell them to multiply the 12,345,679 by 36 (4 x 9)

$$
\begin{array}{r}
12,345,679 \\
\underline{36} \\
74,074,074 \\
\underline{370,370,370} \\
444,444,444
\end{array}
$$

Just remember the magic number 9. Multiply the number they give you by 9, from then on it works itself, and you will always finish up with nine of the number given to you.

PART SIX

THE APPLE AND ORANGE ILLUSION

The effect of the apple and orange illusion is very strong indeed, and the props required are of the type that can be acquired almost immediately. Two paper bags are shown to be completely empty. An apple is placed into one of the bags and an orange is placed in the other. On the word of command, the apple and the orange change places. Both bags are crushed up and tossed aside.

To prepare the apple and orange illusion, you will need the following: two paper bags (these should be of the type with a flat bottom so that they may be stood up on the table; a large size sugar bag would be ideal). You will also require one apple and two oranges. Do not use large size fruit because they are awkward to handle.

The apple and one of the oranges should be almost exactly the same size and the other orange should be just a little larger. Take the large orange and cut it in two, right through the middle. Place one half aside as you will not be needing it. Scoop out the other half of the orange until it is empty, making sure that it is quite clean inside.

This empty half-orange can now be fitted over the real orange and if it is held in the hand with this half facing the audience it will appear to be the same as any other orange. If the half-orange is placed over the apple and held in the same way, no one will know there is an apple behind it.

Project

Perform the illusion

To perform the apple and orange illusion, you start off by having the two bags on your table with the apple and the orange with the half orange over it inside one of the bags. The other bag is empty.

Lift up the empty bag and hold it so that the audience can see right inside it, and replace it on the table to your right. Pick up the other bag and place it on your left palm and reach inside and remove the orange, still with the half-orange over it, and place this fruit into the bag that is on the table. Reach into the bag again and bring out the apple, and place this also into the bag on the table. Now show the bag in your left hand to be empty. Place this bag on the table to your left.

Explain to your audience that you want them to watch very carefully what you are about to do. Reach into the bag on your right and, unknown to your audience, remove the half-orange from the orange and place it over the apple. Bring it out from the bag with the half-orange facing the audience. They will think it is the orange. Place this into the bag on your left. At this point

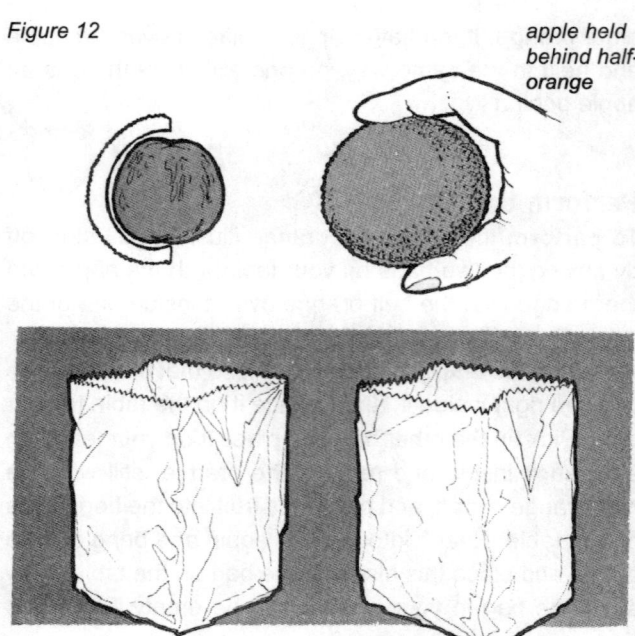

Figure 12

*apple held
behind half-
orange*

ask the audience if they have been watching carefully. They will naturally answer, 'Yes.' When they do, ask them what you have done, and they will tell you that you have taken the orange from one bag and placed it into the other.

'Right,' you reply. 'The orange is over here on my left, and the apple is over here on my right.' As you say these words, lean over the bags slightly and look into them as if confirming that what you are saying is correct.

Actually the trick is over at this point as far as you are concerned technically. It is now a case of presentation. Pick up your magic wand and wave it first over one bag and then the other. Replace the wand on the table and say, 'Watch.' Reach into the bag on your left and bring out the apple, leaving the half-orange in the bag. Place the apple on the table, crush up the bag still containing the half orange, and put it aside. Pick up the other bag, tip it upside down and allow the orange to fall out on to your left hand. Allow the inside of the bag to be seen casually before you crush it up and toss it aside.

Afterwards, your audience, in trying to recall all that you did, will assume that they saw the insides of both paper bags both before and after the effect.

PART SEVEN

THE CUT AND RESTORED RIBBON ILLUSION

This trick is a classic magic effect that dates back several hundred years. It is simple, direct and very easy to perform. All that is required is a length of ribbon, a pair of scissors, and some glue or paste.

To prepare for the effect, take a short piece of ribbon, which should be not more than 7.5 centimetres (3 inches) long, and bend it into a loop as in figure 13 and stick the ends together with glue. Try to make a neat job of it, without ragged edges. The ribbon, incidentally, should be 2.5 centimetres (1 inch) wide. Once you have made this loop, thread it on to a longer piece of ribbon, about a metre long, until it reaches the centre. A pair of scissors at hand is all the preparation that is required.

Project

Cut and restore the ribbon

To perform the effect. Have the ribbon with the loop threaded on to it lying on your table in a position so that the audience cannot see the small loop. The scissors should be lying alongside the ribbon.

Pick up the ribbon with your left hand, with the fingers curled around the small loop. Explain to your audience

Figure 13

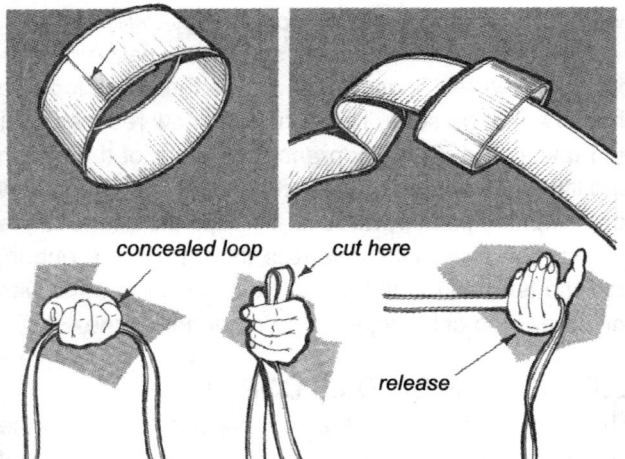

concealed loop   cut here

release

that you are about to show them a magic effect with the aid of this piece of ribbon. As you are saying this, the left hand is held steady at about chest height and the right hand pulls the end of the ribbon that is on the right side downwards until the left end is pulled up nearly to the left hand. Once it has nearly reached the left hand, the right hand should stop pulling the end of the ribbon. Release it and then start pulling down the other end of the ribbon.

In other words, you are apparently aimlessly pulling a long length of ribbon back and forth through the left hand as you are talking to the audience. Pull the ribbon a few times and bring it back to its original position so that the two ends are hanging down more or less together.

Now turn the left hand over so that it is palm upwards but keep the left fingers curled over the small loop so that it cannot be seen. The right hand now reaches over and takes hold of the loop *and* the centre of the ribbon and lifts them up and off the left hand. The left hand now turns with the palm inwards and grasps the centre of the ribbon. The right hand releases its grip on the ribbon, and the left hand is left holding the ribbon in a fist with the small loop only projecting from the top of the fist.

CUT THE TOP OF THE LOOP

The right hand picks up the scissors and cuts away the top of the loop, leaving two ends of ribbon sticking out from the top of your left fist. The audience can now see two ends of ribbon at the top of your fist and another two ends hanging down at the bottom of the ribbon, and therefore think there must be two pieces of ribbon. You have apparently cut the long length of ribbon into two halves. In reality, of course, all you have done is cut the small loop of ribbon. The long piece is still intact. Now you have apparently to restore the cut ribbon into one long length again. To do this, you say, 'We have now cut the ribbon into two pieces. Probably some of you are thinking that I did not really cut it? I will do it again.'

At this point you cut another piece of ribbon from the top of your fist, then another piece, and still another, so that the audience can see lots of small pieces of ribbon fluttering to the floor. What you are really doing at this point is trimming away *all the small loop* until your left hand is holding nothing but the centre of the long piece of ribbon. Once you have trimmed away all the small loop, put the scissors aside and step forward just a little.

'Watch,' you say. 'A miracle is about to take place before your very eyes.'

Take hold of one end of the ribbon and lift it up until it is at right angles to the other end. Keep a firm grip on this end with the right fingers. Start rubbing the fingers of the left hand together and slowly open them. The length of ribbon will drop and will be seen to be one long piece again.

Never hurry this effect. Practise it a few times before you attempt to perform it before an audience. You will realise that every time you perform this effect, you destroy a loop of ribbon, so it is a good idea to make up a dozen or so loops at a time to save yourself the trouble of making one up every time you wish either to practise or perform the cut and restored ribbon.

PART EIGHT

THE CHANGING BAG

The changing bag is one of the most useful props in the magician's repertoire. It can be used for literally dozens of different effects. It can vanish things, it can be used to produce small articles, and it can also be used to exchange one thing for another.

It is simply a cloth bag measuring approximately 20 centimetres (8 inches) across the top by 25 centimetres (10 inches) deep. It has a division across the centre of it so that you can place your hand on either side of this division and it will enter a different pocket on either side. The best changing bags are usually made of a good quality velvet, with a silk or satin lining. It really has two linings, of course, one for each division of the bag.

To explain simply what can be done with a changing bag, drop a table tennis ball into the bag. Now place your right hand into the bag, but into the other side of the divider. Grasp the lining firmly and pull it out so that you are turning the bag inside out. The bag will appear to be empty. The ball has vanished. Turn the lining inwards again so that the bag is back to its original condition. Wave your hand over it. Then reach into the bag and produce the ball again. To produce the ball you simply place your hand into the right side of the divider, the one into which you placed the ball in the first instance.

Have you got the idea? Right! Supposing you place a red ball into the bag before you begin your performance. You can now pick up the bag and turn it inside out to show it to be empty. Turn it back to its original condition, drop a white ball into the bag, wave your hand over it, reach in and produce the red ball. The white ball has apparently changed colour. You can now, if you wish, turn the bag inside out again to show that it is empty.

Once you have grasped the basic idea of the changing bag, very many effects are possible.

Figure 14

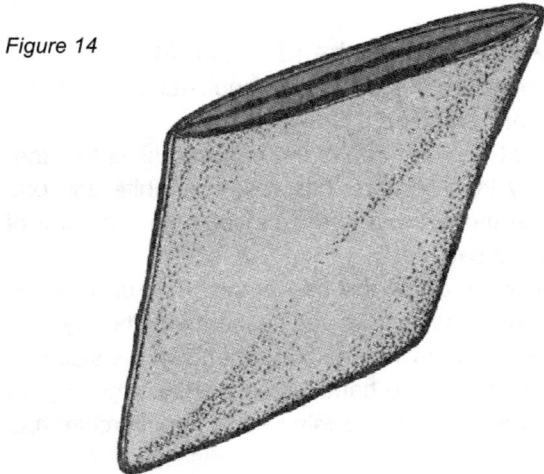

Project

Tricks with the changing bag—Blendo

Place a Union Jack flag into one side of the bag. You will also require three silk or chiffon handkerchiefs—one red, one white and one blue.

To perform. Show the bag empty. Place the three handkerchiefs into the bag, making sure that they go into the pocket that does not contain the Union Jack. Wave your hand or your wand over the bag. Reach into the bag and produce the Union Jack. Show the bag empty. The three handkerchiefs have blended together to make a Union Jack.

Twenty-first-century handkerchiefs

You will need for this effect six handkerchiefs: two red, two white and two blue.

Preparation. Tie three of the handkerchiefs together in a line by their corners: one red, one white and one blue. Place these three handkerchiefs into one side of the changing bag.

To perform. Show the bag empty. Pick up one red and one blue handkerchief and tie them together by their corners. Place them into the bag, but not in the side that contains the first three handkerchiefs. Place the bag on the table. Pick up the remaining white handkerchief and tuck it into your left fist and make it disappear. (Do you remember your handkerchief vanisher?) Pick up the bag and, reaching into it, produce all three handkerchiefs tied together in a line. The white handkerchief that disappeared has somehow magically become tied between the two that were placed into the bag.

The magic sweet shop
Preparation. Place a number of sweets, each one wrapped in its own wrapper, in one side of the bag.

   To perform. Show the bag empty. Place a number of sweet wrappers into the bag, once again making sure that they go into the side of the bag that does not hold the sweets. Wave your hand over the bag, reach in and produce the wrappers but this time each wrapper contains a sweet. This is a particularly strong effect if performed for young children.

PART NINE

IMPROMPTU MAGIC

Impromptu Magic is the title given to the type of trick that can be performed almost at the drop of a hat. Suppose you are out at a party and someone who knows you are a magician asks you to show the guests a trick, you have to be prepared to stand up and do just that. You have to be able to perform 'impromptu', without any special preparation beforehand.

There are two basic types of impromptu magic. The first, and by far the best, requires a high degree of skill and dexterity, and is usually called 'close up magic' by magicians. Many magicians, particularly in the United States, specialise in this type of entertainment. They perform in night clubs and restaurants, or will come to your home if you are having a private dinner party, where they will sit at your dinner table and make your eyes pop with nothing other than their two hands.

One of the most famous was a man by the name of Albert Goshman from Hollywood, California, in the United States. Mr Goshman specialised in coin tricks. He did other things too, but coin tricks were his speciality. He made them appear, disappear, multiply, penetrate the table top, change from copper to silver, all 'before your very eyes', because, remember this, he was sitting there at your dinner table.

Ken Brooke from London was another magician who specialised in this type of magic. He was probably Britain's leading light in this field. More than most people, he had the ability to make people laugh, and when this ability is combined with almost perfection in the art of sleight of hand, you have a world-beating combination.

So the time arrives when someone does ask you to do a trick for them. Your special apparatus is at home, you have not brought anything with you because you did not expect to have to do anything to entertain anyone, so what do you do?

You perform 'impromptu', which means that you use whatever there is to hand. The few tricks that follow are designed with this in mind. One or two of them are of the 'puzzle magic' type, in that they are items that you can do but when a spectator tries he or she cannot do them.

Project

Topsy-turvy glasses

Three glasses are set in a row on the table. The two outer glasses are upside down and the centre one is right way up. The problem is to turn over two tumblers at a time, using both hands and in three moves only, so all three glasses are the right way up.

Remember, three moves. You can turn over the two outside glasses and do it in one move, but ask them to try it in three moves. They must not turn over the same two glasses twice. Each turn must be done with two different glasses.

First of all, you must demonstrate that it can be done, and this you do. Having done it once, offer to do it again, in slow motion, just in case anyone has not quite got the hang of it.

Having done it twice, or even three or four times, you invite a spectator to have a go. But no matter how often he or she tries to duplicate your moves, they cannot get all three glasses the right way up in three moves.

There are two reasons why the spectator cannot follow what you are doing, but before giving these, perhaps we had better explain how you do it.

Set the three glasses up in a row on the table, the centre one right way up and the two outer ones upside down. As they are facing you, take the two glasses on the left, one in each hand, and turn them over. Now cross your arms and turn over the two outside glasses. Now once again turn over the two glasses on the left. That is it. You have done it (see figure 15).

Why, you may ask, is it impossible for a spectator to

Figure 15

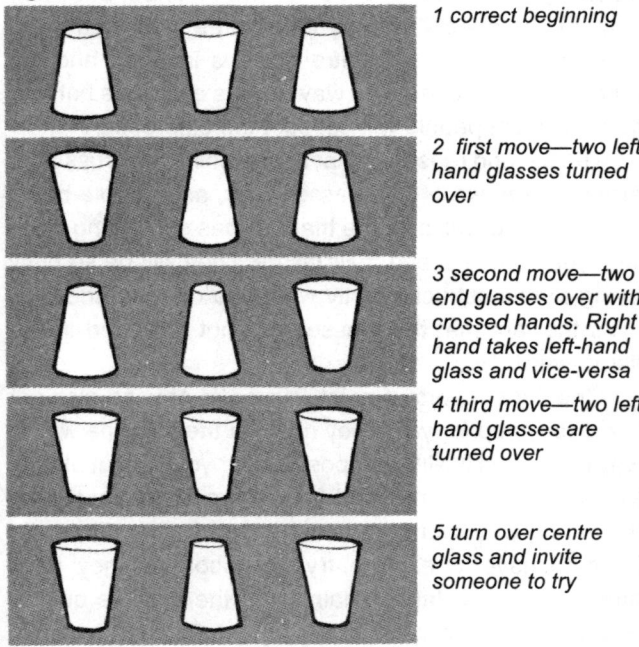

1 correct beginning

2 first move—two left-hand glasses turned over

3 second move—two end glasses over with crossed hands. Right hand takes left-hand glass and vice-versa

4 third move—two left-hand glasses are turned over

5 turn over centre glass and invite someone to try

duplicate this? The first and most important reason is this: having done the effect once or twice, *you* finish up with all three glasses right way up on the table. Having done this, you *turn the centre glass upside down* and ask a spectator to try his or her luck. Have you noticed the difference? When you did it, you started with the centre

59

glass right way up and the other two inverted, but when you ask the spectator to try it the three glasses are the other way round. The centre glass is inverted and the outer glasses are the right way up. It is a strange but true fact that most people will not spot the difference.

The second reason is that at one point you cross your arms to turn two of the glasses over, and people being what they are, will assume that this has something to do with your success and their failure. They will be so busy trying to reconstruct exactly what you did, that they will miss the fact that the glasses are not arranged in the same way.

One very important point. *Never* let anyone else set the glasses up for you. They may set them up the wrong way round and it will be impossible for you to do it. If they try it a couple of times and fail, then set the glasses up the wrong way round and ask you to do it again, invite them to have 'one more try'. As soon as they have attempted it and failed again, grab the glasses quickly and arrange them in the correct order. Do the trick once more, and when all three glasses are the right way up, turn the centre one over and invite them to have just one more try.

You need not use glasses. Any three similar objects that have a top and bottom can be used, but somehow, tumblers seem to be the ideal things to use for this.

Project

The marvellous matches

This is another effect in which you do something that is so simple that it can drive your friends crazy trying to repeat what you have just done. The props used are of the simplest variety: two matchsticks, nothing more.

Place a matchstick into the crotch of your thumb and hold it there. Now place the other matchstick into the crotch of the other thumb and hold this one also. Let your friends see exactly how you are holding them.

What happens now, as far as the spectators are concerned, is that you bring your two hands together and take hold of the two matchsticks between the first finger and thumb of each hand and pull the two matchsticks right through each other. It really looks as if one matchstick penetrates the other.

To perform, proceed in this way. One matchstick is held in the crotch of each thumb. The right hand approaches the left hand, and the right thumb and first finger grip the matchstick in the left hand. Now the left first finger and thumb grip the matchstick in the right hand, but in a slightly different way. The left thumb grips the end of the matchstick that is farthest away from you, and the left first finger curls under the right thumb and grips the end nearest to you. You can now separate your hands and you will be holding a matchstick in each hand.

You can invite anyone to try this and he or she will be unable to duplicate what you have done and will usually end up with the two matchsticks against each other, unable to separate their hands.

Project 🔍

The magic matchbox

This trick can be made up in no more than two minutes and is one of the best impromptu tricks.

To prepare. All that is required is a matchbox, which is prepared in the following way. A small slit is cut with a sharp knife along one edge of the tray of the matchbox. Figure 16 shows this. That is all the preparation needed for the magic matchbox.

The effect is simple. You show a matchbox. Open the drawer and place a five pence coin into the box. You close the drawer of the box. Give the box a shake, and your spectator will hear the coin rattling inside the box. Hand over the box and ask your spectator to open the box and when he or she does so, they will be surprised to find that the five pence has changed to a ten pence coin.

How is it done? The illustration gives the game away. When the five pence coin is placed into the box it is pushed through the slit and straight out into your left hand. The box is closed immediately and shaken to

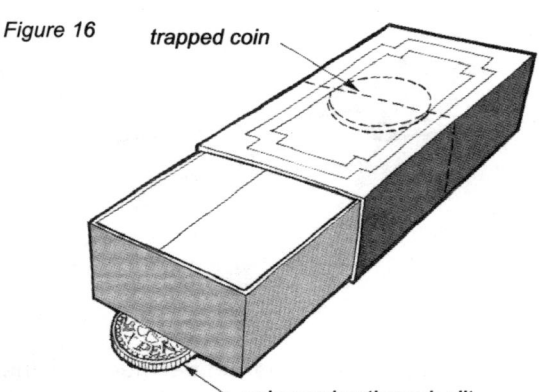

Figure 16

trapped coin

coin coming through slit

allow the spectator to hear it rattling. Actually, the coin that your spectator can hear rattling is the tenpenny piece that, as you will see from the illustration, is trapped between the top of one end of the drawer and the outer cover of the box. As soon as the drawer is closed the coin drops into the drawer.

Project

The broken and restored matchstick

Unlike the topsy-turvy glasses or the marvellous matches, this effect does require a little preparation, but the preparation is so simple and easy to do (figure 17).

The effect is that you take a matchstick and place it in the centre of your handkerchief. Fold the corners of

Figure 17

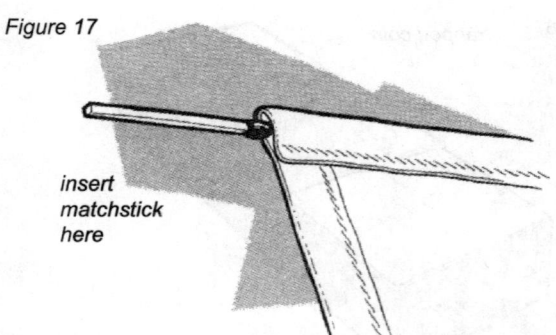

insert
matchstick
here

the handkerchief inwards to the centre then fold the
handkerchief in half and half again, and keep folding it
until the matchstick is well and truly wrapped up in the
handkerchief. Ask a spectator to try and feel the
matchstick through the folds of the handkerchief. The
spectator does so and says that he or she can feel the
matchstick.

Having made sure that the spectator really can feel
the matchstick, ask him or her to take hold of the
matchstick with the fingers of both hands. The spectator
will find this easy to do if you tell him or her to grip the
matchstick with the first finger and thumb of both hands.
When the spectator has a firm grip on the matchstick,
ask him or her to break the matchstick in two.

Once the matchstick has been broken, place the
handkerchief on the table and slowly unfold it. Explain

that when you have completely unfolded the handkerchief you should find two halves of a matchstick. Your audience will naturally agree with you, especially the one who actually broke the matchstick, but when the handkerchief is completely unfolded, the matchstick is seen to be in one piece. It has become magically restored to its original condition.

This is one of the most beautiful little tricks to witness and is very simple to perform. You should have guessed by now that two matchsticks are used.

To prepare. Beforehand, one matchstick is pushed into the hem of the handkerchief. That is all the preparation required. Push it about 5 or 6 centimetres (2 or 3 inches) into the hem to make sure that it cannot fall out prematurely.

To perform the trick, you start off by spreading your handkerchief out on the table. Borrow a matchstick from someone and place it in the centre of the handkerchief. You now fold the handkerchief up. Start by folding the four corners inwards, then folding the handkerchief in half. It does not really matter how you fold it, so long as you keep track of the matchstick in the hem. While you are folding, keep your fingers on this matchstick.

Once you have completed the folding, ask the spectator to feel the matchstick through the folds of the handkerchief. As you say this, you push the handkerchief towards the spectator and guide his or her fingers to the matchstick that is concealed in the hem. Once the spectator has a grip on it, ask him or her to break it. From now on it is simply a matter of making sure that the spectators have understood what has taken place. Point home to them the fact that the matchstick has been broken in two and that when you unfold the handkerchief you should find the two halves. Unfold the handkerchief slowly, pick up the matchstick and hand it to someone. Pick up your handkerchief, shake it out just in case someone thinks there is something under it on the table. Fold it up and place it back in your pocket.

Project

The good-night banner

This is the perfect trick to bring a magic show to a climax. In theatrical terms 'it has everything'. It is a good trick, it is baffling and it tells your audience that the show is over, giving them a perfect cue to applaud.

The effect, as the audience sees it, is like this. Show a piece of black cloth, about 45 centimetres (18 inches) square, to be perfectly blank on both sides. Lay it flat on your table, then pick up a length of ribbon and pile it up on to the centre of the black cloth. Take the front edge of the cloth and fold it backwards over the ribbon. Now pick the cloth up from the table by taking hold of all four corners, which are now at the rear, away from the audience. Walk forward and give the cloth a shake. The front half of the cloth drops downwards and the ribbon, instead of falling on to the floor is seen to be attached to the cloth and forms the words 'Good Night'.

To prepare this effect you will need three pieces of black cloth, each piece measuring 45 x 45 centimetres (18 x 18 inches). All three pieces should be sewn together, as in figure 19. The piece that is shown standing up in the illustration becomes a movable flap. It helps a little if you sew two small lead weights into the two corners, although this is not absolutely necessary. Before sewing these three pieces together, a length of ribbon is sewn to one of the pieces in the form of the words 'Good Night'.

You will see that it is possible to hold the banner up so that the flap is hanging down and the words 'Good Night' are visible, but if you hold the flap up at the top two corners, the banner will appear to be blank.

To perform. Have the banner lying on your table with the flap on top and to the rear half. The words 'Good Night' are within the flap and are not visible to the audience. Pick up the banner by the two rear corners holding the flap also. Show that the banner is blank. Replace the banner on the table, with the *flap at the front edge of the table*.

Pick up a length of ribbon and pile it up on the centre

Figure 18

of the banner. Fold back the two front corners, bringing the flap also. Pick up the banner in this folded condition, holding it by the corners, and step forward. Give the banner a slight shake and as you do so allow the front piece of cloth to drop, exposing the 'Good Night'. The flap is held up at the top and the ribbon is held inside the flap.

By now you will have realised that it is possible to blend two effects together into one. By performing the cut and restored ribbon trick first (*see* page 48), you can then use the ribbon for the good-night banner trick. The best colours to use are either black or dark blue for the banner and white or yellow for the ribbon.

LET'S INVESTIGATE!

Titles in this series: